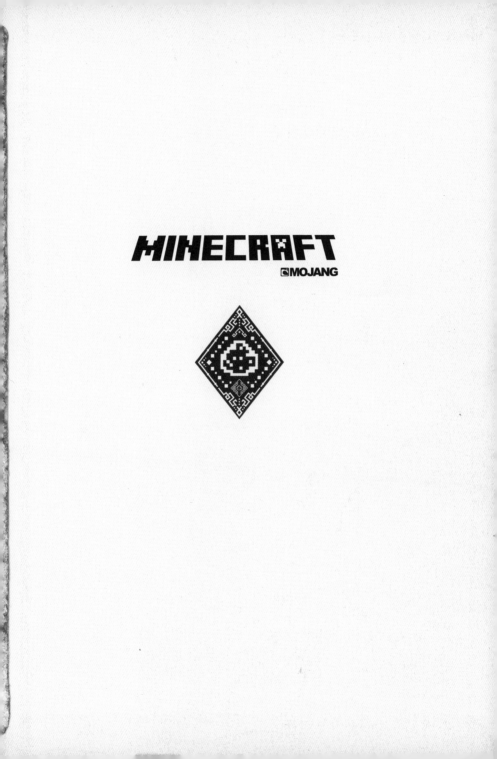

MINECRAFT

MOJANG

EGMONT

We bring stories to life

First published in Great Britain 2013 by Egmont UK Limited
The Yellow Building, 1 Nicholas Road,
London W11 4AN

Written by Nick Farwell, AKA CNB Minecraft
Designed by Andrea Philpots
Concept design by Steffan Glynn
Edited by Jane Riordan and Stephanie Milton
Illustrations by James Burlinson, Theo Cordner, Cubehamster,
SethBling, JL2579 and FVDisco
Production by Louis Harvey and Caroline Hancock.
With thanks to the testing crew: SethBling, Ali, Bella, Jack, Roman, Adam,
William, Isaac and Oscar.

© 2014 Notch Development AB

'Minecraft' is a trademark of Notch Development AB

ISBN 978 1 4052 6840 0
55907/11
Printed in Italy

MIX
Paper from
responsible sources
FSC
www.fsc.org
FSC® C018306

Egmont is passionate about helping to preserve the world's remaining ancient forests.
We only use paper from legal and sustainable forest sources.

This book is made from paper certified by the Forest Stewardship Council® (FSC®),
an organisation dedicated to promoting responsible management of forest resources.
For more information on the FSC, please visit www.fsc.org. To learn more about
Egmont's sustainable paper policy, please visit www.egmont.co.uk/ethical

**Stay safe online. Any website addresses listed in this book are correct at the
time of going to print. However, Egmont is not responsible for content hosted by
third parties. Please be aware that online content can be subject to change and
websites can contain content that is unsuitable for children. We advise that all
children are supervised when using the internet.**

MINECRAFT

MOJANG

REDSTONE HANDBOOK

CONTENTS

WELCOME TO REDSTONE

AN INTRODUCTION TO THE ELECTRIFYING WORLD OF REDSTONE!

Whether you're playing in Survival or Creative mode, redstone is an amazing substance that will open up the immense possibilities of Minecraft. It will enhance your gameplay by teaching you how to connect and control the blocks that make up your world.

Redstone dust and torches were first introduced in Alpha. Repeaters were introduced in the official redstone release Alpha 1.3.1, when it also became possible to obtain redstone by trading with villagers. Witches, who sometimes drop redstone, were introduced in Alpha 1.4.2, followed by pistons in Alpha 1.7. Version 1.5 (AKA 'The Redstone Update') was released in March 2013.

Since its arrival a huge redstone community has developed, building and sharing creations as diverse as arcade-style games, intricate traps, calculators and even computers.

NOTE FROM THE AUTHOR: Most serious redstone creators use the PC/Mac Edition, but many of the builds in this book can be created on the Xbox 360 Edition as well, so go ahead and give them a try!

The first section of this handbook gets you up to speed on the basics of redstone. The second section pushes you to use your new redstone knowledge to complete challenges, and the final section showcases some of the awesome community creations that are out there and gives a little insight into how they work.

SO LET'S GET WIRED UP AND GO CREATE!

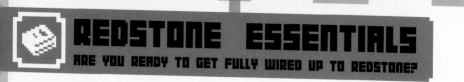

REDSTONE ESSENTIALS

ARE YOU READY TO GET FULLY WIRED UP TO REDSTONE?

REDSTONE ORE

Redstone ore is the raw, mineable block from which you get redstone dust. When mined in the PC/Mac Edition with an iron, gold or diamond pickaxe, each block of redstone ore will drop four or five pieces of redstone dust.

WHERE TO FIND IT

Redstone ore is found deep underground, within 1 to 16 blocks of the bedrock layer. Time to get mining, then! Just remember the Number One Rule of Minecraft: never dig straight down.

REDSTONE ORE

If you're playing in Creative mode you'll have an infinite supply of redstone at your fingertips. If you're playing in Survival, the easiest way to get to redstone ore is to find a cave system that leads deep underground. This will save you digging your way down by hand and should lead you straight to a nice supply of redstone ore.

ENCHANTING YOUR TOOLS

When mined with an enchanted fortune pickaxe, a block of redstone ore will drop up to 8 pieces of redstone dust.

ENCHANTMENT TABLE RECIPE

Can be used to enchant tools, weapons and armour in the safety of your own home.

You can enchant your tools on an enchantment table. To craft a table you'll need 4 blocks of obsidian, 2 diamond gems and 1 book. This is an expensive investment, but an enchanted fortune pickaxe will pay for itself many times over when you start mining redstone, diamond and emerald.

DID YOU KNOW?

A block of redstone can be used as a power source. See pages 16–17 to find out more!

REDSTONE BLOCK RECIPE

A redstone block can be crafted from 9 pieces of redstone dust.

REDSTONE DUST

Redstone dust is really powerful stuff and is essential to almost all redstone circuits. Take some time to get to grips with it now and you'll be glad you did later!

Within a circuit, redstone dust acts like a wire. It carries a redstone signal from a power source to another redstone item, such as a repeater, a piston or a door.

USING REDSTONE DUST

You'll need to place the dust on top of a block, not on the sides or the bottom. Placing several pieces of dust next to each other will create a wire. Simple!

TIP: Remember, redstone dust can't help you until you've given it a power source.

PROPERTIES OF REDSTONE DUST

Redstone dust is pretty clever. You can run it up and downhill to create a wire without the connection breaking. Just remember that it can't travel vertically more than one block at a time.

But, clever as it is, the dust still needs to be told what to do. You need to direct it into the item you want to power. Simply placing an item (e.g. a piston) next to a wire and giving it power won't do the trick. The end of the wire must be pointed at the item you're trying to power.

When the dust receives a signal from a power source, it can send that signal a maximum distance of 15 blocks before it runs out of strength. At that point you can place a repeater at the end of the wire to make the signal last for another 15 blocks. (Turn to page 13 to learn about repeaters.)

REDSTONE TORCH

You'll want to familiarise yourself with this handy item. A redstone torch has several uses and, amongst other things, can act as a power source in a redstone circuit.

HOW A REDSTONE TORCH WORKS

A redstone torch is turned on by default, so when it receives power or a redstone signal it actually turns off. Unlike a lever or a button you can't switch it on and off by hand.

Redstone torches are an essential ingredient for redstone repeaters (see opposite page), redstone comparators and activator rails.

Redstone torches have a 1 tick (0.1 second) delay when they are switched on or off. When used in long chains they can cause a few seconds' delay which you should factor into your calculations.

REDSTONE TORCH RECIPE

You can craft a redstone torch from just a stick and a piece of redstone dust.

TIP: Redstone torches have a light level of 7 which is half the light output of a regular torch. They won't melt ice or snow, and don't try using them as a mob-spawning deterrent or you'll be in for a nasty surprise ...

 DID YOU KNOW? A tick is an amount of time, and in redstone terms it refers to the time it takes the signal to travel from the power source to the object you are trying to power. A 1-tick delay is 0.1 seconds, a 2-tick delay is 0.2 seconds and so on.

REDSTONE SECRETS

A redstone repeater is a very useful item. Once you've wired it up the possibilities are endless!

HOW A REPEATER WORKS

A repeater will accept a signal at the back and then push it out of the front with renewed signal strength. For reference, the back of the repeater is the side closest to you when you place it.

A repeater has several functions, but the two most important are:

1 To increase the distance a redstone dust wire can send a signal. When added to a circuit, the repeater takes a signal of any strength and refreshes it so that it is repeated at full power (hence its name).

2 To create a delay between receiving the signal and outputting the signal. This is the most important function as the delay is critical to complicated machinery that requires specific timings to work correctly, such as a piston door. The maximum delay that can be created by a repeater is 0.4 seconds, but you can use several repeaters to create longer delays.

By default, the repeater delay is set to 1 tick, but it can be changed to 2, 3 or 4 ticks by hitting the use item button when the repeater is in place. You'll notice the torch moves along each time you hit the repeater, signalling that you've changed the tick.

PISTON

Pistons may just be the most revolutionary addition to redstone because they allow redstone circuits to physically move the blocks around you. When given power, a piston can push the blocks in front of it.

PISTON RECIPE

You can craft a piston using wooden planks, cobblestone, an iron ingot and redstone dust.

DID YOU KNOW?
One piston alone can push up to 12 blocks at a time, and it can push them in any direction.

5 pistons, each pushing 12 blocks.

STICKY PISTON

Sticky pistons are often more useful than regular pistons. They can pull a block backwards as well as pushing it forwards. When a sticky piston receives power it will push a block forwards, and when it stops receiving power it will pull the block backwards.

Sticky pistons powered by levers, pulling and pushing blocks.

STICKY PISTON RECIPE

You can craft a sticky piston using a regular piston and a slimeball.

When killed, big slimes divide into small slimes, and small slimes divide into tiny slimes. It's only the tiny slimes that drop slimeballs.

POWER SOURCES

T orches aren't the only power source available to you. There are several other interesting ways to power a circuit. This table shows the different options for powering up with redstone.

	Redstone torches		Levers		Detector rails
	Redstone blocks		Pressure plates		Trapped chests
	Buttons		Tripwire hooks		Daylight sensors

WHAT POWER SOURCES DO

Power sources provide a redstone signal to other redstone items like redstone dust, pistons and TNT.

A lever providing a redstone signal to a piston.

USING POWER SOURCES

With the exception of the redstone block, trapped chest and daylight sensor, a power source needs to be attached to a regular block before it can work.

The power source will then send out a signal for 1 block in all directions except diagonally.

The easiest way to use a power source is to place it next to the item you want to power, since all power sources send power to the blocks next to them. Buttons, levers, pressure plates, tripwire hooks and detector rails also power the block to which they are attached, and anything that is next to that block.

TURNING POWER SOURCES ON AND OFF

A lever can be toggled on and off, allowing you much more control over your circuits and machines. The only power source that can't be turned off is a redstone block.

SENDING YOUR REDSTONE SIGNAL IN A SPECIFIC DIRECTION

As you now know, a power source sends out a signal in all directions except diagonally. However, if the power source is next to redstone dust or a repeater, you can use those items to direct it wherever you want it to go.

... CONTINUED

We've looked at a few power sources already, but here are some additional power source recipes that will come in handy for the upcoming challenges!

WOODEN BUTTON

Produces a 1.5-second redstone signal when pressed

Must be attached to a block

Can be activated by arrows (they will keep the button pressed)

STONE BUTTON

Produces a 1-second redstone signal when pressed

Must be attached to a block

Cannot be activated by arrows

Replace the wood with stone for a stone button.

WOODEN PRESSURE PLATE

Produces a 1-second redstone signal (unless constantly pressed down)

Can only be placed on top of a block

Can be activated by a player, animal, monster, minecart, boat or dropped item

STONE PRESSURE PLATE

Produces a 1-second redstone signal (unless constantly pressed down)

Can only be placed on top of a block

Can only be activated by a player or monster, not dropped items

Replace with stone for a stone pressure plate.

WEIGHTED PRESSURE PLATE

Can only be placed on top of a block

Can only be activated by a dropped item

Produces a 1-second redstone signal (unless constantly pressed down)

Amount of items dropped onto pressure plate increases its redstone signal strength

Replace the iron with gold for a gold weighted pressure plate.

LEVER

Must be attached to a block

Can be toggled on and off by the player

Produces a constant redstone signal

TRIPWIRE HOOK

Must have a second tripwire hook opposite (2 blocks or more away)

Produces a 0.5-second redstone signal (unless constantly pressed down)

Connected with string to the other tripwire hook

Will react to players, monsters, animals, minecarts, boats and dropped items

Must be attached to a block

LIGHTING SYSTEM

You wouldn't think twice about switching on a light in your own home, but in Minecraft even that simple action requires a redstone circuit, and creating that circuit is up to you.

TIP: We suggest that you try out the challenges in this section of the book in Creative mode while you get used to working with redstone. That way you'll have access to all the materials you need.

REDSTONE LAMP RECIPE

You can craft a redstone lamp using redstone dust and glowstone.

REDSTONE LAMP LIGHTING SYSTEM – THE BASIC IDEA

You can create a basic redstone lighting system using redstone dust, a lever and a handful of redstone lamps. Let's create one for this simple log cabin.

During the day, the log cabin is lit by natural light coming in through the windows. But when darkness falls, monsters spawn inside, causing no end of trouble! To solve the problem, you need a way to keep the inside of the cabin lit at night. Instead of lighting it with regular torches, you can use redstone to create a more sophisticated lighting system.

By placing a strip of redstone lamps in the ceiling and connecting them to a lever, you can create a light switch that can be switched on and off as you desire, depending on the time of day.

Simply connect the redstone lamps together by running redstone dust along the top of them, then run that dust to the block that your lever is attached to.

This is a fairly basic redstone circuit: a power source (lever) powering another object (redstone lamp) from a distance, using redstone dust to carry the signal between the two items.

LIGHTING SYSTEM
... CONTINUED

N ow that you've got to grips with the principles of a basic circuit, it's not a great leap to increase its usefulness by adding some extra features. Ready?

REDSTONE LAMP LIGHTING SYSTEM WITH SENSORS

By replacing the lever in your redstone lighting circuit with a daylight sensor block, you can make your lighting system come on automatically when it's dark and turn off again when the sun rises. Clever, eh?

DAYLIGHT SENSOR RECIPE

You can craft a daylight sensor from glass, nether quartz and wood slabs.

> **DID YOU KNOW?** A logic circuit uses a certain combination of inputs to produce a specific output, and can be used when you need something a little more complicated than a simple on/off function. A NOT gate is a type of logic circuit that changes the output of an item so that it has the opposite effect. This can come in handy in redstone circuits, as you're about to see.

1

Clear a 4 x 1 opening in your roof. Fill that space with redstone lamps, then place a daylight sensor next to the lamps, with a 1-block space between them. This picture shows the ideal placement.

2

Place a block 1 space away from the sensor and put a redstone torch on the side closest to the redstone lamps. This is your NOT gate. Finally, lay down redstone dust between the block and the sensor.

3

To complete the circuit, run redstone dust along the top of the lamps. Although the torch isn't directly next to the redstone, it still counts as an entire block, so the circuit is complete.

4

Usually a daylight sensor emits a signal if it's light. The effect of the sensor has now been changed by the NOT gate, so that it emits a signal when it's dark, powering the circuit and switching on the lamps.

A beautifully illuminated home and not one switch in sight!

PISTON DOORS

Piston doors are a very popular redstone contraption that open as if by magic, and constructing one is a great way to learn about all the vital elements of redstone.

SLIDING DOOR

TIP: Bear in mind that when you place a sticky piston, its sticky side will be facing towards you.

DID YOU KNOW?
You can't place blocks directly on top of redstone dust, but you can place them one block higher.

1

Build a 3 x 3 block arch with a 2-block empty space in the centre for the doorway. Then place 2 sticky pistons to the right of the door, facing inwards, and place 2 blocks in front of them.

Redstone creators often use different coloured wool blocks to signal different parts of their circuits. The different coloured wool blocks make it easier to see how the circuits are created, so we have used this method throughout the book.

2

Dig down 2 blocks behind the pistons. Place a block of blue wool in the hole and a redstone torch on top of it to create your NOT gate.

3

Place another block on top of the torch, then place redstone dust on the top. This dust will be enough to power both of the pistons. That's the door finished!

4

Dig a 2-block deep trench running round from the blue wool block to the front of the door. Run redstone dust along the bottom of the trench right up to the door. This will allow you to connect a pressure plate to the pistons.

5

Fill in the top layer of your trench with blocks of your choice and place a pressure plate in the doorway so the door can be triggered open. Because of the NOT gate, the pressure plate causes the pistons to open the door instead of closing it, which is far more useful.

6

To make your door open from either side, dig another identical trench from the back of the door to the pistons, and place another pressure plate inside. Now hide your circuitry with extra blocks.

WARNING: A piston door activated by a pressure plate can be a great way to welcome guests to your home, but don't forget that pressure plates can be activated by foes as well! Is that a zombie in the living room?

Uh oh, ZOMBIES!

MINE CART STATION

Before the introduction of horses, minecarts were the only way to travel in style, and they are still a popular mode of transport. You can use redstone circuits to make minecarts even more exciting.

BASIC MINECART STATION

You will need powered rails and a track switcher to create a basic minecart station. The powered rails get the minecart moving fast, and the track switcher allows you to select your destination station.

MINECART RECIPE

Smelt 5 blocks of iron ore in a furnace to give you 5 iron ingots, which will make a minecart.

RAIL RECIPE

16 basic rails can be crafted from a stick and 6 iron ingots.

POWERED RAIL RECIPE

You can craft 6 powered rails from a stick, redstone dust and gold ingots.

1

Create an L-shape of blocks in a large open space. It should be 2 blocks high, 3 blocks down and 5 blocks across.

2

Build a 1-block high T-shape in the middle of your L-shape, then add a 2-block high pillar next to that. Place a lever on the far left, on the bottom block.

3

Place a button on the 2-block high pillar. You'll be able to reach this from your minecart. Now build a T-junction (a junction where two tracks meet), by placing 3 powered rails followed by 4 regular rails. Add stairs leading up to your rails.

4

Dig a trench 1 block below the main curved track. Dig 1 more block down, and fill that space with light blue wool blocks as shown above. Then add one more blue block on top, as shown. Finally run redstone from behind the lever to the last blue block.

DID YOU KNOW? At top speed, minecarts move at 8 miles per hour. They will move further if they are carrying someone or something.

5

Dig a 1-block deep trench underneath the junction so you can get to the wool block. Now place a redstone torch on the side of the wool block facing the junction. This torch will act as your signal for switching tracks.

6

Fill in the trench and complete your track so that it has 2 destinations. When you pull your lever, your junction will switch position. Now the fun can begin: set down your minecart on the rails, get in, push the button and you're away!

TIP: When you run over a powered rail that is switched off, a frictional force is applied which is usually enough to stop your minecart. You can use powered rails that are switched off to create more stations along your track.

ADVANCED MINECART STATION

One day, with a bit of practice, an advanced station like this could be yours! It has several interesting features: multiple destination selection, selection lights, selection sounds, separate arrival and departure tracks and a minecart dispenser.

The concept is similar to the basic station in that it uses a power source to switch the T-junctions and select the destination station, but it uses a different button system to allow you to pick your destinaton.

PULSE SHORTENER

The pulse shortener, or monostable circuit, is one of the most important logic gates used in complex redstone machines. It allows you to keep something switched on for a certain amount of time.

> **DID YOU KNOW?** The usual delay between activation and reset of a power source is just 0.1 seconds/1 tick. This is deliberately short, so that it can be combined with a sticky piston to create a toggle flip-flop (see pages 34–35).

A pulse shortener is the starting point for many redstone creations. You can use it to control how long a door stays open or how many arrows are fired from a dispenser.

POWERED TRAPDOOR

This example shows a pulse shortener in use with a trapdoor. The circuit is toggled on so that the trapdoor is shut, then when something walks over it, you can flip the switch and the trapdoor will flip open quickly. Gotcha!

Dig a 2-block wide hole and fill it with light green wool. Then, place 2 repeaters, facing away from the wool. Set the left repeater to 4 ticks by hitting the use item button, and leave the right one set to 1 tick.

Place a sticky piston next to the 4-tick repeater, facing right, and attach a block of blue wool to it as shown.

2

Dig a hole next to the blue wool block and place another blue block in the hole. Place a lever next to the green circuit.

Place redstone dust as shown in the image. The circuit in this example is connected to a trapdoor with a hole beneath, but the choice of mechanism is up to you.

3

When you pull the lever back to activate the circuit, the trapdoor will open for a short period of time (the exact time will depend on the number of ticks set). Then, when the piston pushes the blue block out, the circuit will be broken and the trapdoor will close again.

In this example the trapdoor opens and shuts quickly. If you add more repeaters on the back row you can keep it open for longer.

TRAPDOOR RECIPE

You can craft a trapdoor to catch your enemies using 6 wooden planks.

TOGGLE FLIP FLOP

No, not that kind of flip-flop! The toggle flip-flop is another important circuit. It provides a redstone signal that can be toggled on and off.

A toggle flip-flop is especially useful when you want to use a button instead of a lever to activate mechanisms like doors.

The example below uses a sticky piston T flip-flop design. What a mouthful! The signal arrives into the circuit, then the flip-flop circuit toggles its output on. If you send another signal to the circuit it will toggle its output off.

1

Create a circuit of 2 light green wool blocks, placed 1 block apart from each other. Place a sticky piston facing upwards in the middle of the wool blocks.

2

Put another wool block on top of the piston. Then place redstone dust on the block on the left and a repeater facing away from the middle on the block on the right.

3

Place a sticky piston (facing right) next to the repeater, 1 block up. (You'll need to place a block below it first, then destroy it.) Attach a block of redstone to the sticky piston. Finally, place a button on the side of the green block on the left and dust on the floor, as shown.

4

Press the button and the sticky piston on the right will push out the redstone block, powering your redstone wire. Press it again and the piston will pull the block back, disconnecting the circuit.

This is a toggle flip-flop being used to power a piston door (as featured on pages 24-25). The flip-flop powers the circuit when it is turned on. And, because it toggles, you don't have to dash through before it slams shut in your face!

35

CLOCK CIRCUIT

Clock circuits are used to create pulsing signals for a variety of machines, from alarms to arrow launchers. It might not sound like the most exciting tool, but it's the starting point for creating some really cool stuff!

REDSTONE TORCH 3-CLOCK

A torch clock is a series of redstone torches strung together that continually turn one another off. The result is a pulsing output signal that switches on and off repeatedly. This example is called a 3-clock, because there are 3 on and 3 off ticks between each pulse. You can make clocks with more torches, but you must always use an odd number of torches in the loop to allow each torch to turn the next torch off before it is turned off itself. If you use an even number of torches, half of the torches will be permanently switched on and the other half permanently off. Not very useful!

1

Find an open space and build this light green wool circuit. The circuit is made up of 2 blocks with a 2-block trench between them, with 2 blocks filling the trench.

2

Repeat step 1 to create another green line as shown above. Add redstone torches, then add a trench of blue blocks to join up the green circuits. Link the torches together with redstone dust.

FROM BASIC 3-CLOCK TO ARROW DISPENSER

You have now built a basic 3-clock. The next steps show you how you can use this circuit to make an arrow dispenser, which is a super-cool and highly useful weapon.

DISPENSER RECIPE

A dispenser can be crafted from 7 cobblestone blocks, 1 redstone dust and 1 bow.

TIMED AUTOMATIC ARROW SHOOTER

3

Place a block next to the corner of the blue circuit, then a dispenser on top. Put redstone dust on top of the dispenser. (See the tip below.) Now place another single block next to the dispenser with redstone dust on top to link the circuit.

TIP: As with a sticky piston, when you place a dispenser it will be facing towards you. Make sure you're facing in the opposite direction to the way you want it to dispense.

4

Put a lever on the side of one of the blue blocks to turn the circuit on and off. Fill the dispenser with arrows, hit the lever and let 'em fly!

Players of the PC/Mac Edition will discover that it isn't possible to put redstone on a dispenser simply by right-clicking on it, as this will open the dispenser. Hold down shift as you right-click to place redstone dust. Remember, this won't work if you're flying.

BLOCK CIRCUITS

... CONTINUED

REPEATER CLOCK

A repeater clock is made of 2 repeaters passing a signal around in a constant loop. To prevent the repeaters simply powering each other on, it is started by a 1-tick signal from a pulse

shortener, which ensures the repeaters are only on for 1 tick before turning off again. They pass the signal around in a loop while continually turning on and off, which means your arrow dispenser will now pack some serious fire power. Enemies, beware!

1

Find a clear space and place 4 blue blocks in a square, with another block to the side. This last block will be the extension that you need for looping.

2

Place 2 repeaters on top of the blue wool facing in different directions and a line of redstone from the top repeater. Now add the green circuit above with a repeater facing left, a sticky piston facing up with a block on top, and finally a block with redstone on top next to that.

3

To add the toggle, create the floating pink circuit next to the highest green block. Place a sticky piston facing left (towards the repeaters), a block on the back with a lever on top, and a block in front.

4

Add a staircase of blocks in front of the 2 repeaters. Place a dispenser on the top and add redstone dust as before. This completes the circuit.

5

Add plenty of arrows to your dispenser. Pull the lever and the arrows will shoot out incredibly fast. This one is guaranteed to scare your enemies away!

REDSTONE CHALLENGES
GET READY TO TRY YOUR FIRST REDSTONE CHALLENGE!

DELUXE LIGHTING SYSTEM

This seriously cool lighting system doesn't just turn your lights on and off, it physically moves the light source in and out of the room using a block swapper. A challenging build, but great fun and well worth the effort.

CONSTRUCTION MATERIALS

Switched off/ switched on

1

Clear a space above your selected room. It will need to be at least 5 x 3 blocks. The light will sit flush with the ceiling so you won't have to change the way the ceiling looks. You'll just need to make a hole in the ceiling where you would like the glowstone light to appear when you turn the switch on.

2

Place 3 green wool blocks in a row, just behind your hole, then add an extra block at a diagonal at each end.

3

Add a redstone torch on top of the central green wool block, and place two repeaters on either side of this torch. They should be pointing away from the torch and directed into the 2 blocks at either end. Now add a redstone torch to the side of these 2 blocks (not on top).

4

Place a regular piston directly below the redstone torch on the left, so that it faces the hole in the ceiling. Then add a sticky piston 1 block above the ceiling, facing down towards the hole, so that the blocks can slide past it before being pushed into the roof. This can be tricky to place, so place 3 blocks above the hole, then remove the lowest 2. Jump down the hole, look upwards and place your sticky piston on the underside of the green wool.

5

Add a regular ceiling material block to the right of the sticky piston, then fill the hole in the ceiling with a glowstone block, ensuring it touches the sticky piston face. Then add one more piston facing towards the regular ceiling material block.

6

Decide where you'd like the on/off switch to sit inside the room and place either a lever or a button there. Remember to connect your lever/button to the main circuit. Try this vertical torch circuit to save on resources.

CLASSIC JEB DOOR

Despite its name, the Jeb Door wasn't actually created by Jeb himself. Jeb (Jens Bergensten) is the lead developer of Minecraft and he discovered this design on the internet when pistons first went live in-game.

The design has changed dramatically over time but the basic idea is still the same. The door is hidden from view when closed and sits flush with the wall. When activated it slides across to reveal a secret passageway.

CONSTRUCTION MATERIALS

8 · 12 · 16 · 2 · 1 · 8 · 4

1

Find a location for your door. This example uses a cliff, inside which you will create a hidden room. Now decide how you would like to open the door. There are several options, but the simplest way is to use a lever hidden nearby and connected to the door.

2

Place the lever at your chosen location. For the door itself, you will need an area 6 blocks wide, 4 high and at least 3 blocks deep. If you can make your space deeper, you'll find it easier to install your door.

3

Establish the centre of your space and create a 2 x 4 block pathway down the middle, using stone brick. Place 4 sticky pistons on each side of your space in a 2 x 2 formation, as shown above, with 4 blocks of space between the pistons on each side. These pistons will slide the door aside once it's been pulled back from the wall.

4

Now place 2 more sticky pistons on each side; they should be facing out towards the front of the clear area and stacked on top of each other. Place a block in front of each of these pistons. Make sure these blocks are the same material as the wall (smooth stone in this case).

5

Place a blue wool block above each piston, and two more in the middle. Then place a repeater on each side facing outwards. Make sure each repeater is set to a 2-, 3- or 4-tick delay as 1 tick won't work. Place redstone dust on top of the remaining blocks to connect the pistons together.

6

Test the system by placing a lever near to the middle and turning it on. The door should extend out into the cliff wall and sit flush against it. After testing, remove the temporary lever. (You will be using the hidden lever that was placed in step 2.)

Your lever now needs to be connected to the redstone on the door. Just run a redstone dust wire from the door to the lever. Make sure the wire is connected in the central area at the top of the door. This ensures that both sides of the door are powered.

Finally, cover up the door mechanism. You can then build a room, a base or anything else you like behind your very own secret entrance!

LAVA PIT TRAP

This trap is difficult to spot, reacts extremely quickly and is almost impossible to escape from! It works by pulling the floor out from beneath another player when they open your trapped chest, then it drops them into a pool of lava. Ouch!

DID YOU KNOW?

A trapped chest is a chest that emits a redstone signal from all sides when opened and is a great anti-theft device.

CONSTRUCTION MATERIALS

TRAPPED CHEST RECIPE

A single trapped chest can be crafted from a chest and a tripwire hook. Place 2 trapped chests next to each other to create a large trapped chest.

1

This trap needs a small corridor, below which the pit will be hidden. Dig your corridor at least 5 blocks long, 2 wide and 3 high.

Dig your lava pit. It should be 3 x 2 blocks and 3 blocks deep. Add a large trapped chest to the end of the corridor. It will need to sit on 2 blocks.

2

At this point, you'll need to temporarily destroy the walls of the corridor to build the redstone mechanics. To create the sliding floor, place 3 sticky pistons on each side of the pit, as shown.

3

Now put blocks in front of the pistons; these will be the floor of the corridor. In this example we've used stone brick to help blend the trap into its surroundings.

Place a blue wool block above each sticky piston and then run redstone along the tops. This will power all the pistons on each side so they slide out simultaneously.

4

To connect the chest, dig down 1 block on either side of it so that you can see the blocks on which the chest is sitting. You now need to place redstone torches on the sides of the blocks the chest is on.

5

Hide the torches with stone blocks (the torches will power them and the floor will slide back into place). To connect that power to the pistons, place a block of wool next to the stone block and put redstone dust on top of both of them (on both sides).

6

Test your trap by standing in the corridor and opening the chest – you should fall into the pit.

7

Finally, fill the pit with lava and build up the walls of the corridor to hide the redstone.

The next person who tries to steal your stuff is in for a scorching surprise!

DUAL SHOT CANNON

This cannon is a modified version of a regular TNT cannon, which fires TNT at your enemies. The dual shot cannon uses a small timing circuit at the back to dispense a second block of TNT into the cannon before it fires, giving the cannon double the power for every shot. Your enemies aren't going to know what's hit them!

DID YOU KNOW?

A TNT cannon works on the principle that TNT will not destroy blocks when it explodes in water. By sitting blocks of TNT in a water bed, the cannon will not explode on itself, but will still fire another TNT block in the direction it is facing.

CONSTRUCTION MATERIALS

13 8 8 7
1 1 1 1
5 5 1

1

Place a fence post with a wooden pressure plate on top. Build up 3 blocks on the right, then 2 blocks on the left with a dispenser on top, facing towards the 3-block tower.

2

Lay a row of 4 blocks on the ground, heading away from the pressure plate. The TNT will be fired from the pressure plate and the water will sit along the row of blocks.

3

On the right of this water bed, but 1 block higher, place a row of 4 dispensers all facing inwards. Mirror this with a row of 4 blocks on the left. Remember, you'll need to hold down shift to place floating dispensers next to each other in the PC/Mac Edition.

4

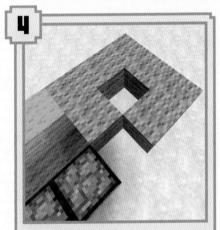

Create this pink timing circuit. This is a 3 x 3 square with a hole in the middle and a block missing from one corner as shown.

5

Place redstone dust along the top of the dispensers (see tip on page 37). Then, in the corner of the pink circuit where the block is missing, place a sticky piston facing upwards, with a pink block on top. Place 4 repeaters set to 4 ticks on top of the pink blocks as shown. Connect them with redstone dust.

6

Add a chain of repeaters leading from the pink circuit to the dispenser at the front. Make sure they are all set to 4 ticks of delay so that the TNT can travel a decent distance before exploding.

7

Fill the central water bed with water. Now place a button on the side of one of the dispensers (any of them will do, just remember to hold down shift if playing PC/Mac Edition) and fill all 5 dispensers with TNT. Your cannon is now ready to fire so give it a try. KABOOM!

SUPERCHARGED FIRE ARROW LAUNCHER

This amazing machine allows you to shoot flaming arrows out of a dispenser at a rate of 5 per second, at the mere press of a button. That should keep those hostile mobs at bay!

CONSTRUCTION MATERIALS

'Is it just me, or is it getting hot in here?'

1

Create a 3 x 3 square of blocks of your choice, with a 1-block space in the middle. Place another block behind the square in the centre, and place a dispenser on top of that. Make sure it's facing in the direction you want to fire.

2

Place a fence gate in front of the hole. You'll need to place another block below it first, then destroy that block when the gate is in place. Hit the use item button to open the gate. It doesn't matter whether the fence gate opens inwards or outwards.

3

The gate acts like a solid block and will allow you to fill the hole with lava without it spilling out of the front.

Place the lava here.

TNT

WARNING: Adding the lava can be tricky: make sure you place the lava behind the fence gate and aim for the spot marked in the image. Be especially careful if you're playing in Survival mode. If you pour lava all over yourself you're going to have a meltdown ...

SUPERCHARGED FIRE ARROW LAUNCHER

... CONTINUED

4

To make the arrows fire from the dispenser at high speed you'll need a super-fast clock circuit. Place 4 blocks on the level below the dispenser as shown.

5

Add a piece of redstone dust at each end and two repeaters in the middle: one facing into the dispenser and the other facing the opposite way. This forms the clock circuit.

6

To make the circuit turn on and off at the push of the button, you need a simple piston-based pulse shortener, as shown in green. Then add the button onto the side of the frame.

7

Next, add 4 pink blocks: 2 blocks should be placed at ground level at a diagonal to each other, and 2 more blocks one level above the ground, also positioned at a diagonal to each other.

Place redstone dust on the ground-level pink block furthest from the dispenser and a redstone repeater on the other ground-level pink block (facing towards the dispenser). Add a sticky piston to the side of the pink circuit as shown, then add a single pink wool block in front of that sticky piston. Finally, fill your dispenser with arrows, then hit the button and you're away! Just hit the button again when you want to turn it off.

Two arrow launchers positioned behind the walls of a fort. Nobody's getting in here ...

COMMUNITY CREATIONS

CHECK OUT THESE IMPRESSIVE COMMUNITY CREATIONS!

14 FLOOR ELEVATOR

The 14 Floor Elevator created by Cubehamster is one of the most impressive single-task redstone contraptions ever made. It allows you to travel to 14 different floors in a super-fast piston elevator. Now that's travelling redstone style!

The player accesses a user interface at each level to select which floor they want, in much the same way as a real elevator.

 CUBEHAMSTER: This well-respected redstone expert is a teacher of physics and chemistry based in the Netherlands. He's never been known to turn down a challenge!

PISTON ELEVATOR

The concept behind the moving part of the elevator is pretty simple. The design is 2 blocks wide and the player needs to stand right in the middle of 2 pistons. The player is pushed up by a piston on the left, then a piston on the right, and this process is repeated until they reach the desired floor.

This concept was originally showcased by the player Brows of Steel and has since become the standard mechanism for many piston elevators.

FLOOR SELECTION

Although the moving elevator part is simple, the circuitry that allows you to select a floor is a whole new level of complicated!

Like a real elevator, there is a different button to press for each floor. Each button sends a redstone signal when pressed. These signals vary in length depending on which button they have come from, so the elevator can work out which floor has been chosen by detecting the length of the signal.

INSTANT CALL FUNCTION

One of the best things about this elevator is that the player doesn't have to wait for the elevator to arrive at their floor. In fact, it's quicker than elevators in the real world. When the player selects a floor by pressing a button, the signal is sent directly to the floor that he's on and the elevator is immediately ready for use.

SUMMARY

In version 1.5.2, this piston elevator was the pinnacle of elevator design. None could match its speed and efficiency. Although this design was too big and too complicated to create in a Survival game, Cubehamster also created a simpler, more practical elevator design that transported a player one floor at a time. He really did think of everything!

COLOUR MAP DISPLAY

You can't tell at first glance, but this enormous redstone contraption creates an image so large that it can only be viewed on a Minecraft map.

MAP DISPLAY MECHANICS

The map works out which colour occurs most often within each 2 x 2 block area, and uses that dominant colour for 1 pixel. Viewed from above, the machine has 1 wood and 1 stone block in each cell. The redstone pushes 2 more blocks into play, and that determines the colour of the pixel. When you look at the Colour Map Display on a map you'll see it's formed an image, like this one of Notch. Amazing!

PISTON PIXEL CHANGERS

You can programme several different images into the machine. Devices called piston loops arrange blocks in the display area until the image has been prepared. It can then be viewed on a map. You can change the image at the push of a button: when you hit it, the piston loops push new blocks into place and the new image is ready to view on your map.

REDSTONE

It's the redstone's job to shift all of the piston loops around at the same time. This is done from a single button!

SUPER STOPWATCH

This super stopwatch created by JL2579 and Cubehamster is an amazing piece of redstone engineering. It can record time to a 10th of a second, faster than the blink of an eye!

It uses a super-fast memory array to measure the time and a compact decoder system to display the numbers on a 4-digit display. It has 2 buttons, one to start and stop the timer, and one to reset the time after it has been used and recorded.

JL2579: JL specialises in amazing redstone and piston creations, as well as big farms. He's particularly interested in pushing the boundaries of what's possible in Survival mode to their very limits.

For more creations from JL2579 check out: www.youtube.com/JL2579

SUPER-FAST REPEATER LOCK MEMORY ARRAY

The driving force behind this stopwatch is a unique memory system which is used to store and record the numbers that are then displayed on the 4-digit display.

This system uses the repeater lock function. When you hit the stop button, the repeaters lock the time that is currently on the display. When you hit the button again, the clock continues from that time. The repeater lock can process information very quickly. This is essential for a stopwatch since it is recording units of time smaller than 1 second.

DID YOU KNOW? This kind of clock display is called a 7-segment display. Much like an LED clock in the real world which has 7 LED segments for each number, this clock has 7 redstone lamp segments for each number.

DECODER

The special memory array needs a special decoder to display the numbers using redstone lamp segments. This clever redstone component uses what's known as a slide system to display different numbers.

The slide system pushes sets of blocks (arranged vertically to save space) into the path of constantly powered repeaters. When a block that allows a redstone signal to pass through it is pushed into place, the signal from the repeater is sent down a line of redstone that goes directly into the back of the corresponding segment of the display and lights it up.

But this system has one small drawback: because the slide system then has to be pushed back up into its default position, it can't change state fast enough to keep up with the super-fast repeater lock memory array that drives it. So, the 10ths of each second are only displayed after the stop button is pressed.

SUMMARY

JL's stopwatch is a fantastic example of a high-end redstone machine. The concept isn't unique, but the way in which it delivers its timekeeping is. This is one of the most compact stopwatches ever created.

DID YOU KNOW? Stopwatches like this one have been used in numerous mini-games and adventure maps to time laps and tasks set during the adventure. Check out FVDisco's Sonic the Hedgehog™ map – it's a great example.

69

GOLD RUSH

Gold Rush is a redstone mini-game that's big on fun! The idea is to control a villager in a minecart, leading him to several chutes to collect gold bars, while avoiding the TNT that also drops into the chutes. It's explosive fun!

The player stands on a platform and moves a minecart by stepping on and off a pressure plate. You can change the direction of the track using a lever. You can choose to play one of three levels of difficulty: TNT can fall in either one, two or three of the four lanes.

CNB: AKA Nick Farwell, is based in the UK and is well respected for his redstone tutorials.

PISTON LOOPS AND 7-SEGMENT DISPLAY SCOREBOARD

The player's score is stored in a piston loop. This is a selection of blocks that is continually moved around by pistons. The blocks turn redstone lamps on or off, depending on which type of block is in play: glass or a solid block. Glass doesn't allow a redstone signal to pass through it and so gives an off state, whereas a solid block does allow the signal through and so the lamp is turned on.

TIP: If you want to get high scores, play on the highest level of difficulty.

GOLD RUSH
... CONTINUED

REDSTONE RANDOMISER

This machine is used to randomise the chutes that the gold and TNT fall into, and it does this by detecting when a chicken runs onto a pressure plate!

Every time a chicken activates a pressure plate, the plate emits a signal which is sent to a piston loop that controls which chutes the TNT and gold drop into. It takes several chickens inside the randomiser to generate a high number and a variety of drops from the chutes.

SUMMARY

The mechanism behind Gold Rush is a tangle of piston loops and logic gates. It uses clocks, pulse shorteners, AND gates, NOT gates, transistors and T flip-flops!

It's a complex design, but when you break it down it's simply a collection of common redstone components that have been linked in an incredibly clever way to create an awesome redstone machine.

ZOMBIE SIEGE

Zombie Siege is a fun combat mini-game. The player must defend their base from hordes of zombies that are lumbering towards it by firing at them with a bow and arrows and TNT cannons. Who said a zombie apocalypse couldn't be fun?

The first few rounds are a nice, easy warm up for the player, but once you hit double digits the difficulty rapidly ramps up. At this point your cannon aim has to be bang on target if you want to survive.

TNT CANNONS

The TNT cannon on each side can be fired to 3 different ranges, allowing you to blow up zombies virtually anywhere on the map. They are controlled by 3 buttons (one for each range). Cleverly, they use the same piece of redstone dust to carry their separate signals; by placing each button 1 block further away from the cannon, the machine can work out how far the signal has travelled and therefore which

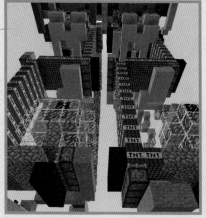

button has been pressed. Depending on which button it is, the game loads different amounts of propellant TNT into the cannon to control the range of the block of TNT that's actually being fired.

DID YOU KNOW? In order to stop the zombies catching fire in the sun for this game, FVDisco had to construct an enormous sheet of ice and position it in the sky above.

◼◼◼◼◼◼◼ ◼◼◼◼◼◼

... CONTINUED

7-SEGMENT LEVEL DISPLAY

The level display shows you which round of the game you're currently playing. There are 99 rounds in total, but nobody has ever made it that far!

ZOMBIE CONTROLLER

As in Gold Rush, the zombies are spawned randomly by a chicken walking over a pressure plate, which sends a signal to a dispenser and a mob egg. The number of dispensers increases with each level you pass, meaning there are more zombies to kill.

To encourage the zombies to walk in the right direction, Disco uses villagers in minecarts under the floor! Zombies can sense targets through solid blocks even if they can't see them, and will head for the villagers.

The minecarts carrying the villagers need to move fairly slowly so that the zombies don't lose interest. Disco uses wiggly tracks to slow the minecarts down.

SUMMARY

Zombie Siege uses a combination of TNT cannons and traditional weaponry, along with huge waves of marauding zombies to create a brilliant mini-game.

The redstone circuitry behind the game involves some imaginative techniques. The variable range cannon was one of the first to be made and used in a game so successfully. The simple single-range version has since become the standard design for TNT cannons.

HINTS AND TIPS

We spoke to the experts themselves to get their tips on working with redstone. Here's what the Mojang team had to say:

- Working with redstone can be frustrating, but stick at it! It's very satisfying to see your creation function as intended after all your hard work.

- If your redstone creation includes TNT, wait until everything else is placed before placing the TNT. It's far less dangerous that way.

- Try testing out your designs in Creative mode before making them in Survival.

- Building is more fun with friends. Your parents might come in handy, too!

- Focus on getting your creations to work properly before making them more compact or more attractive.

- We're still adding new features! Just because you can't do something now, doesn't mean you won't be able to do it in the future.

- Do not build redstone creations next to water. It'll mess up your plans!

USEFUL LINKS

Check out this list of useful websites. They'll really extend your Minecrafting experience.

Official Minecraft website:
www.minecraft.net

Official Mojang website:
www.mojang.com

The Minecraft wiki:
www.minecraftwiki.net

The official Facebook page:
www.facebook.com/minecraft

Mojang Team's YouTube channel:
www.youtube.com/teammojang

The official Minecraft Twitter page:
https://twitter.com/mojangteam

Notch's official Twitter page:
https://twitter.com/notch

Jeb's official Twitter page:
https://twitter.com/jeb_

Egmont's Minecraft website:
minecraft.egmont.co.uk

Here are some other Minecraft sites, not monitored by Mojang or Egmont. Enter at your own risk!

Creative community fansite Planet Minecraft:
www.planetminecraft.com

The Skindex – for all your Minecraft fashion needs:
www.minecraftskins.com

Minecraft on Reddit:
www.reddit.com/r/Minecraft/

Disco's YouTube channel:
www.youtube.com/FVdisco

SethBling's YouTube channel:
www.youtube.com/sethbling

JL2579's YouTube channel:
www.youtube.com/JL2579

(See page 2 for our 'Stay safe online' policy.)